Marcus Garvey

Sandra Donovan

Raintree
Chicago, Illinois

For information, address the publisher:
Raintree, 100 N. LaSalle, Suite 1200, Chicago, IL 60602

Printed and bound in the United States at Lake Book Manufacturing, Inc.
07 06 05 04 03
10 9 8 7 6 5 4 3 2 1

Library of Congress Cataloging-in-Publication Data

Donovan, Sandra, 1967-
  Marcus Garvey / Sandra Donovan.
     p. cm. -- (African American biographies)
Summary: Profiles Marcus Garvey, a self-educated black man who worked to end world-wide discrimination against Africans, to help black Africans regain control of their countries, and to promote black pride, unity, and power.
Includes bibliographical references (p.) and index.
  ISBN 0-7398-6870-5 (HC), 1-4109-0038-X (Pbk.)
 1. Garvey, Marcus, 1887-1940--Juvenile literature. 2. African Americans--Biography--Juvenile literature. 3. Universal Negro Improvement Association--Juvenile literature. [1. Garvey, Marcus, 1887-1940. 2. Civil rights workers. 3. African Americans--Biography. 4. Universal Negro Improvement Association.] I. Title. II. Series: African American biographies (Chicago, Ill.)
  E185.97.G3D66 2003
  305.896'073'0092--dc21

2002153359

Acknowledgments
The publishers would like to thank the following for permission to reproduce photographs:
pp. 4, 26, 34, 36, 42 Underwood & Underwood/CORBIS; pp. 6, 8, 12, 17, 20, 24, 28, 33, 41, 47, 49 Bettmann/CORBIS; p. 10 Rykoff Collection/CORBIS; pp. 14, 44, 51, 53 CORBIS; p. 22 David J. & Janice L. Frent Collection/CORBIS; p. 39 The Mariners' Museum/CORBIS; p. 50 The Marcus Garvey and UNIA Papers Project, UCLA; p. 54 Hulton/Archive by Getty Images; p. 57 Hulton-Deutsch Collection/CORBIS; p. 58 Jacques M. Chenet/CORBIS.

Cover photograph: Bettmann/CORBIS

Content Consultant
Tamba M'bayo
Department of History
Michigan State University

Some words appear in bold, **like this.** You can find out what they mean by looking in the Glossary.

Contents

Marcus Garvey rides in a parade through New York City's Harlem neighborhood.

Introduction

Marcus Garvey was an important black leader during the first half of the 20th century. He believed that black people would never receive fair treatment in countries where most of the people were white. To give black people a chance for justice, Garvey started a "Back-to-Africa" movement in the United States. He preached that black people everywhere should consider Africa their homeland and that they should settle there.

At the beginning of the 20th century, people of African descent lived in **poverty** in countries around the world. Their families had been kidnapped from Africa and sold as slaves to Europeans many years earlier. By 1900, most of these countries had freed their slaves, but black people continued to live terrible lives.

Although they were free, black people in most countries were treated badly. Often they could not own property or go to school. They usually worked long days at hard physical jobs and were paid very little. Most white people did not see black people as their

A Harlem bookstore hosts a registration for the "Back-to-Africa" movement in 1964.

equals. This was true in the United States and it was also true in many smaller countries. Many former slaves lived in small island countries in the Caribbean Sea, where kidnapped Africans had been brought by boat as slaves.

Most black people did not know that they had a proud history, and many felt worthless. They had been treated badly for so long that many of them had begun to see themselves as second-class people.

This was the environment in which Marcus Garvey grew up in his native Jamaica. But even as a young man, Garvey was not satisfied with this life. He knew that he and his fellow black people deserved to be treated better. He worked his whole life to give pride and power back to poor black people.

Garvey spent his life telling people of African descent to be proud of themselves. He told them that they deserved their own communities where they would not be treated badly by white people. He dreamed of helping millions of black people from around the world return to their homeland. Garvey never even visited Africa himself and his idea of starting an all-black nation never happened. However, he was successful in that he changed the way black people viewed themselves. In the course of his life, he influenced millions of black people across the world, helping them to feel proud of themselves and where they came from.

Marcus Garvey is wearing a cap and gown in his role as President of the Negro Improvement Association. The year was 1921, and he had come a long way from his Jamaican roots.

Chapter One:
Growing Up in Jamaica

Marcus Mosiah Garvey was born August 17, 1887, in the country of Jamaica. Jamaica is an island located in the Caribbean Sea. It has a hot and humid climate that is good for growing crops like sugar cane. When Garvey was born, the island of Jamaica was ruled by Great Britain. It was called British Jamaica.

Garvey was the youngest of eleven children. Both of his parents were full-blooded Africans. Their families had been brought to Jamaica as slaves. In the 1700s, many African slaves were brought to Jamaica. Some were later taken to the United States. Many others, like Garvey's relatives, were sold to British sugar cane farmers in Jamaica.

In 1833, slavery was outlawed in Jamaica. Although former slaves became free, they still had very hard lives. Most of the people who owned land in Jamaica were white Europeans. They

These sugar-cane cutters in Jamaica take a break from hard labor in the fields to pose for a photograph.

also had most of the money. They paid former slaves very little to do hard jobs like working in the sugar cane fields.

Childhood

Garvey's family was dark skinned. In Jamaica, blacks were treated badly by whites. Light-skinned black people also treated dark-skinned blacks badly. But when Garvey was young, he did not know this. He had many friends who were white. They all played together in the small town of St. Anne's Bay.

Garvey's father was a stonemason. He was skilled at cutting stone to make objects. Since he had this skill, he was able to earn more money than many other dark-skinned blacks on the island. He spent most of this money on books. He taught himself about history and the law.

When Garvey was not playing with his childhood friends, he borrowed books from his father. His favorite books were about slave **revolts** in Jamaica. During revolts, slaves would band together against their masters. After many bloody revolts, slaves finally gained their freedom in Jamaica. Garvey loved to read these stories about brave black heroes.

End of Childhood

Two sad things happened to Garvey after he turned 12. First, his father died. Without Garvey's father to earn money, Garvey and his family became very poor. Nine of Garvey's brothers and sisters had died also, so the Garvey family now had only three members. There was Garvey, his mother, and his sister Indiana.

A second sad thing happened to Garvey soon after his father died. A close friend told him she had to stop being his friend. She was white and her parents told her she had to stop playing with Garvey because he was black. This was the first time Garvey realized that some people did not like him because he was black. He was angry and sad. He said later that this ended his childhood.

Garvey worked in a print shop like this one.

Becoming a Printer

When Garvey was 14, he left school to help his family by getting a job. He went to live with his godfather, Alfred Burrowes, to learn to be a printer. In those days, printers operated large **printing press** machines. They printed books and magazines. Burrowes taught Garvey how to use the printing press. He also had a large library of books. Garvey continued to read many books.

Two years later, in about 1906, Garvey moved to the large city of Kingston, Jamaica. He wanted to learn more about the printing business. He went to work for his uncle in a large print shop. This shop printed the large city newspaper. Soon after that he left his uncle's shop to work for P.A. Benjamin Limited, another printing company.

In Kingston, Garvey learned about the newspaper business. He worked all day and read and studied on his own at night. He carried a small dictionary wherever he went. Every day, he studied three or four words in the dictionary. At night, he wrote sentences using the new words.

Becoming a Leader

Garvey was successful at the printing shop. He soon became a boss. In 1907, the workers at the shop went on **strike.** A strike is when workers refuse to work until they get better treatment from their bosses. Workers who get paid very little can go on strike to try to get higher pay.

When the printers went on strike, Garvey was the only boss who took their side. He thought they should be paid more. He thought they were being **discriminated** against because of the color of their skin. The workers' strike did not succeed. When the strike ended, the workers went back to work for the same low pay. However, Garvey was fired because he had taken their side.

Garvey sits at his desk working. He used the money he made from his jobs to travel and fight for the rights of black people worldwide.

Chapter Two:
Traveling the World

Garvey found another good job as a printer, but he was unhappy. He was unhappy about the lives of poor workers in Jamaica. He was unhappy about the **discrimination** faced by black people, especially dark-skinned black people, in Jamaica. He had read many books that said dark-skinned people around the world faced this same discrimination.

Garvey wanted to work to end this discrimination. He needed money to do this kind of work. Since he could not make much money in Jamaica, he decided to travel to other countries to try to earn money. At this time, many black Jamaicans were moving to countries in Central America and South America to find better jobs. Garvey decided to follow them.

First Travels

In about 1910, when Garvey was 23, he sailed for the country of Costa Rica in Central America. His uncle helped him find a job there on a banana plantation. A plantation is a large farm.

Meeting Migrant Workers

When Garvey arrived at the plantation in Costa Rica, he found many other Jamaican workers. He also met **migrant workers** from other countries in the Caribbean Sea. Migrant workers travel around from job to job. Often they work picking fruit during the growing season in one area. When the growing season ends, they move to another area to pick another kind of fruit. Migrant workers usually make very little money.

Garvey was shocked at the living conditions of the migrant workers. They had little to eat and they often slept outside. They usually did not have running water or a place to clean themselves.

The banana plantation was owned by an American company called The United Fruit Company. Garvey was upset that this company treated the workers so badly. The company made a lot of money but the workers did not.

Garvey wanted to help the migrant workers improve their living conditions. He started a newspaper called *The National*. He wrote

These migrant workers in Costa Rica are picking ripe coffee beans from trees on a plantation.

that workers should band together to force their bosses to treat them better. However, the workers were afraid of losing the little money they made. Garvey's newspaper soon failed.

Other Countries

In Costa Rica, Garvey was upset by the conditions he saw on the plantation. He decided to travel more to see what life was like for workers in other countries. He borrowed money from his uncle in Jamaica and traveled to the Central American country of Panama.

In Panama Garvey met **migrant workers** building the Panama Canal. This canal is a huge artificial river that connects the Atlantic Ocean to the Pacific Ocean between Central and South America. Again, Garvey was shocked by how badly the workers were treated, so he started a newspaper. He wrote about the terrible conditions faced by workers. He said it was unfair. Again he told the workers that they needed to **unite** to fight for better treatment. But migrant workers in Panama were also afraid of losing their jobs. Garvey's newspaper soon went out of business.

Garvey decided to visit more countries to see how workers were treated. He traveled throughout Central and South America. He went to the countries of Nicaragua, Ecuador, Honduras, Venezuela, and Columbia. Everywhere he went he saw the same thing. He saw migrant workers suffering bad treatment. They worked long hours in the hot sun and were paid very little.

Fighting For Workers

Garvey decided that he would fight for the rights of these workers. The workers were mostly from Jamaica and other islands that were ruled by Great Britain. About 250 years earlier, Great Britain had invaded these islands and taken control of them. Great Britain sent white people to rule Jamaica and the other islands.

The people living on these islands were then citizens of Great Britain. Citizens are members of countries and should be protected by the country's government. Garvey thought the British government should do something to help the migrant workers.

Garvey traveled back to Jamaica to ask the British government there to do something to protect the migrant workers. The government in Jamaica did not listen to Garvey. He felt they did not care about him or about the workers because they were black. He knew that black people around the world would have to work hard to fight this kind of **discrimination.**

After the Jamaican government refused to help, Garvey made another decision. He decided to go to London to see how blacks were treated there. He hoped to meet people of African descent from around the world and hear their stories. He hoped to find a way to help end discrimination.

African-American educator Booker T. Washington, seen here in 1903, wrote a book that inspired Garvey to act on what he believed.

London, England

In 1912, at the age of 25, Garvey moved to London, England. His sister Indiana was already living there. When Garvey arrived he found a job writing for two newspapers.

In London Garvey met many leaders of the black community. He became interested in the movement to help black people across the world. He read many books. He knew that the countries in Africa were controlled by white Europeans. He wanted to help black Africans take back control of their countries.

Garvey was strongly affected by one book he read in London. The book was called *Up From Slavery*, by Booker T. Washington. Washington was a former American slave who became a leader in the African-American community in the United States. *Up From Slavery* was his autobiography, the story of his life. He wrote that African Americans first needed to improve their own lives, and then they could work toward equal rights in society.

This poster is for a talk by Marcus Garvey. He worked hard to get his message out to as many people as possible.

Chapter Three: Improving Lives

After two years in England, Garvey returned to Jamaica. He was ready to begin his work to improve the lives of black people. He wanted to help black people **unite,** or join together, to achieve this goal.

In Jamaica, as in other countries Garvey had visited, white people were in power. White people **discriminated** against blacks. Garvey was interested in helping black people like himself improve their lives. He started a group called the **Universal Negro Improvement Association (UNIA).** The group's goal was to help black Jamaicans improve their lives. Garvey taught that black people would have to unite to overcome the **discrimination** of white people.

Proud To Be of African Descent

Garvey told black people that if they improved themselves they would win the respect of other people. He said one way to improve

This man in Oklahoma City is drinking from a water fountain that is separate, or segregated, from the fountain white people could drink from. This is the kind of unfairness that made Garvey angry.

themselves was to get an education. He wanted to start schools for black Jamaicans.

Garvey also wanted black Jamaicans to unite with people of African descent living around the world. He said they would be stronger if they joined together. Then they could create their own community and their own governments. They would be free of the **discrimination** of the communities they lived in now. They would

In His Own Words

"I asked, 'Where is the black man's government? Where is his King and his Kingdom? Where is his President, his country, and his ambassador, his army, his navy, his men of big affairs?' I could not find them; and then I declared, 'I will help to make them.'"

"My doom—if I may so call it—of being a race leader dawned on me."

Garvey said this after reading *Up From Slavery*, by Booker T. Washington.

also be free of the discrimination from governments run by white people. Garvey told black people that governments run by white people would never give them power.

Garvey also dreamed that one day people of African descent around the world would return to Africa. At this time, many African countries had governments run by white Europeans. Garvey wanted to return these governments to the African countries. Then he wanted black people from around the world to live in Africa. There he believed they would finally be free from discrimination.

This UNIA parade on August 1, 1922, shows African-American nurses marching through the streets of Harlem.

UNIA's Beginnings

At first, few people joined **UNIA.** The ones who did were the poorest and least educated Jamaicans. Garvey became a leader to these people. He told them to be proud of their African blood. UNIA's motto was "One God! One Aim! One Destiny!" This meant that black people had to **unite** to achieve improvement. Black **unity** is the idea that black people from around the world should join together to be powerful.

Not long after Garvey returned to Jamaica in 1914, he read a book called *Up From Slavery.* This was the autobiography of an American black leader named Booker T. Washington. In his book, Washington said that black people had the responsibility of "pulling themselves up by their bootstraps." He meant they needed to make their own lives better, because they could not expect anybody else to make things better for them.

Garvey was inspired. He promised himself that he would help black people improve their lives. He thought they had been treated badly for so long that they no longer fought against **discrimination.** He thought they needed to act together to fight for their rights.

In August, 1915, Garvey held the first meeting of UNIA. He spoke to a crowd of black Jamaicans. He told them that white people were waiting to see the black people do something for themselves. He said that once the black people helped themselves, they would gain the respect of whites around the world.

Trip to the United States

Two years after he returned to Jamaica, Garvey was ready to expand UNIA. He wanted to bring his message to black people around the world. He needed money to do this.

Garvey decided to go to the United States. He had two reasons for his trip. First, he would try to raise money for UNIA. Second, he would get to see firsthand how African Americans lived and how they were treated. He wanted to bring UNIA to the United States.

Garvey traveled often to spread his beliefs to black people everywhere. In this photo, Garvey is about to sail from Canada to England, where he would start another magazine.

Chapter Four: Success

Garvey arrived in New York in March 1916. Right away he began talking to black people in America. He asked wealthy African Americans for money for **UNIA,** and asked poor African Americans to join UNIA.

Garvey told African Americans the same things he had told poor black Jamaicans. He told them they should be proud of their African blood. He told them they should work hard to improve themselves and earn the respect of white people. And he told them about his dream of black people from around the world moving back to Africa.

When Garvey first arrived in the United States, he stayed in an area of New York City called Harlem. Harlem was one of the world's largest communities of black people at that time. Many black people from the southern United States were moving to the

North. They were moving because there were more jobs in the North than in the South. Many of them found factory jobs in New York and found places to live in Harlem. In this community, Garvey found many African Americans who were interested in his ideas.

In the United States, as in other countries Garvey had visited, most white people **discriminated** against black people, especially in some southern states. White people and black people were forced to live in separate parts of society. They could not eat at the same restaurants, stay in the same hotels, or go to the same schools. They could not even drink from the same water fountains. This was called **segregation.**

One day in June 1917, a community leader from Harlem heard Garvey speaking on a street corner. This man invited him to come speak at a big church in Harlem. This was Garvey's big chance to tell people in Harlem about his ideas. Instead of a few people listening to him on the street, there would be hundreds of people listening to him.

Garvey gave a powerful speech in the church that night. He told African Americans that they needed to join together to become strong. He told them that they would not succeed in a world run by white people. He said they needed to find their own black-skinned leaders.

The Harlem Renaissance

In the 1920s, African-American literature experienced a period of great growth and success. These changes came mostly from writers in Harlem, a part of New York City that had mostly black people living in it. The period was called the Harlem Renaissance, and it proved to everyone that there were talented black writers, as well as leaders such as Garvey, in the United States.

The writers wrote about the experiences of black people living in America. The most famous writers included James Weldon Johnson, Langston Hughes, Nella Larsen, Countee Cullen, and Jean Toomer.

African-American musicians also became popular with whites as well as blacks during this time. An African-American bandleader named W.C. Handy became known as the father of the blues. African-American bandleaders Louis Armstrong and Duke Ellington became the country's leading jazz musicians.

Garvey was an excellent speaker. The crowd loved him. They were excited to hear what he had to say. Black people in Harlem were ready to change their lives in the ways Garvey talked about. They wanted to be proud of their African blood. In just a few weeks, more than 2,000 people joined **UNIA.** Garvey was starting to be successful.

Across the United States

Now that Garvey was getting popular in New York, he wanted to tell his ideas to people across the United States. He went on a trip across the country. His goal was to talk to people about his ideas for black power and black unity. He wanted to get people to join **UNIA.** He also wanted to raise money for UNIA.

Discrimination and **segregation** had been taking place for many years across the United States. By 1919, many African Americans were used to it and even put up with it. But one thing happened in 1919 that made people realize how unfair this was. World War I ended in Europe, and many American soldiers returned home to the United States.

Many of these soldiers were black. In Europe, they had found that they were treated more fairly than they had ever been treated by white people at home. When they returned home to segregation and discrimination, they were angry. After all, they had fought for their country. They knew they did not deserve to be treated unfairly because of their skin color.

In the summer of 1919, this anger led to many **race riots.** During these riots, African Americans and white Americans fought bitterly in the streets of many cities. Many of the fights started when African Americans demanded to use public places where they were usually not allowed to go. People threw rocks at other people

The police in this picture are taking a black man to a safe zone during the Chicago Race Riot of 1919.

and burned buildings. Many African Americans even had their houses burned down. Black people were angry with how they were being treated by white people. White people were angry that black people were demanding equal treatment.

During this time, many African Americans listened to what Garvey had to say. They understood his message of black power and black **unity.** They felt that they would never be treated fairly by white people. They agreed with Garvey that they needed to **unite** to

Garvey was popular because he had strong beliefs that he spread with his moving speeches and slogans. Here he rides in a parade so his followers can see him in person.

become powerful. Instead of feeling ashamed of being black, they began to feel proud. Thousands of African Americans across the country joined **UNIA** and became followers of Garvey's message.

Spreading the Word

By 1919, Garvey was famous across the country. Almost 100,000 people belonged to UNIA. To help spread his ideas, Garvey started a newspaper. It was a weekly newspaper called *Negro World*. In this newspaper, Garvey told black people to be proud of their blood. He told them to find black heroes. He told them to give their children black dolls to play with. He told them that "Black is Beautiful."

People around the world read *Negro World*. Many people started talking about Garvey's ideas. People everywhere were repeating Garvey's slogan: "Black is Beautiful." In Harlem, UNIA had a large headquarters called Liberty Hall.

In 1919, Garvey and his secretary, Amy Ashwood, married. They had a big wedding ceremony at Liberty Hall.

This parade through Harlem in 1924 opened up a convention (a large meeting) that was organized and led by Garvey.

Chapter Five:
Back to Africa

In just a few years, Garvey had become famous across the United States and around the world. Thousands of people were listening to his ideas on black pride, black **unity,** and black power. But these were not his only ideas. Garvey also wanted black peole to have their own nation.

Garvey said white governments would always **discriminate** against black people. He said the only way for black people in America and in the rest of the world to be powerful was to have their own government. Garvey believed that the continent of Africa was the perfect place for black people to set up their own government. It was the homeland from which most black people's ancestors had come.

In those days most countries in Africa had white European governments because they had been taken over by European countries earlier. This is called **colonialism.** Most of the money and land in these colonized countries belonged to the European governments and wealthy white business people. The black people living in Africa were mostly poor and often treated badly by the white governments. Garvey wanted to change this. He wanted black people to rule Africa again. Then, he thought blacks from around the world should move back to Africa. Here they could have their own communities and their own governments. In Africa, Garvey believed, they could be free from **discrimination** and colonialism.

Black Star Line

To travel across the ocean during Garvey's time, people had to take long journeys on large ships called ocean liners. Ocean liners were run by companies owned by white people. Sometimes they did not allow blacks to travel on the ships at all. When they did, they only allowed them to stay in uncomfortable parts of the ship.

Garvey told black people that they did not have to put up with this treatment. He said blacks needed to stop giving their money to whites who **discriminated** against them. He had a plan that would help black people get back to Africa and keep their money in the black community at the same time.

Marcus Garvey wanted to create a company owned by African Americans for black people to cross the ocean.

Garvey's plan was a shipping company called the Black Star Line Shipping Company. This company would own boats to carry black passengers. It would be owned entirely by black people, and would allow them to travel in style. It would keep black people's money out of the pockets of white people who **discriminated** against them.

Garvey opened the Black Star Line in 1919, with a rusty freight ship that was 32 years old. Garvey named his first boat the S.S. *Frederick Douglass*, after a famous African-American hero.

Garvey raised money for his shipping line by selling stock in the company to black people. Stock is a piece of ownership in a company. Five dollars would buy a small part of Black Star Line. When the company started making money, the owners would be paid. Garvey sold stock to hundreds of people. They were proud to be part owners of a company run by people of African descent.

Ship Trouble

Garvey's plan was that black people from around the world would travel back to Africa on Black Star Line ships. In 1920, he bought two more ships for the company. However, the ships he bought were old and could not travel on the ocean. They needed expensive repairs. Garvey spent too much money on them, and soon his company ran out of money. It went bankrupt.

Frederick Douglass

Marcus Garvey named the Black Star Line's first ship after Frederick Douglass (1817–1895). Douglass was one of the most important African-American leaders of the 1800s. He was born into slavery as Frederick Augustus Washington Bailey. Unlike most slaves, Frederick was able to educate himself. In 1838, he escaped from his master  and went to New Bedford, Massachusetts. He was about 20 years old. To avoid capture, he changed his name to Frederick Douglass.

Over the next several years, Douglass gave many speeches about freedom and his life as a slave. He protested against **discrimination.** He was a very strong speaker, and he earned many followers. In 1845 he published his autobiography, and in 1847 he started an antislavery newspaper called the *North Star.*

Douglass argued against discrimination. He worked hard to help slaves escape. During the Civil War (1861–1865), Douglass helped recruit African Americans for the Union Army. Many times he talked about the problems of slavery with President Lincoln. Douglass was a hero to Marcus Garvey and black people around the world because he devoted his life to ending slavery and fighting for black rights.

These parade marchers are opening up the annual "Provisional Republic of Africa in Harlem" convention—a gathering organized by Garvey.

International Convention of the Negro People of the World

Although Garvey's shipping business was in trouble, he was still a popular African-American leader. In 1920, he and his group **UNIA** were famous and powerful. That August, Garvey held a huge meeting for black leaders from around the world. He called it the International **Convention** of the Negro People of the World.

During this convention, Garvey introduced the Declaration of the Rights of the Negro People of the World. This was based on the U.S. Constitution, including a Bill of Rights. Garvey's Bill of Rights said that black people were created equal with other races.

Garvey also made a UNIA flag to fly at this convention. The flag was red, black, and green. Garvey said that red stood for Africans' blood, black stood for the color of their skin, and green stood for their hopes. Today many proud people of African descent around the world still fly red, black, and green flags.

The convention lasted for a month. It included a large parade through New York City. Garvey led the parade dressed in a fancy uniform and a feathered hat. Thousands of followers cheered. At the end of the parade, Garvey gave a speech at Madison Square Garden. He told the thousands of African Americans to be proud and strong. He talked about his idea to create a home for all black people in the African country of Liberia.

W.E.B. DuBois

William Edward Burghardt DuBois was one of the greatest African-American civil rights leaders. He was born in 1868 in Massachusetts. He grew up poor but was able to go to public high school until he was 16. People in his hometown were able to raise enough money for him to go to college at Fisk University. Fisk was an African-American university in Tennessee. DuBois was an excellent student and went on to receive two degrees from Harvard University.

DuBois knew firsthand how difficult life was for many poor African Americans, and he wanted to change this. He became a professor at Atlanta University and wrote books, magazine articles, and newspaper articles.

In 1910, DuBois left his teaching job and started the National Association for the Advancement of Colored People (NAACP). This group was started to make sure the the voice of African-Americans would be heard. Its goal was and is to bring social justice and equal rights to America's black citizens. It has become the largest and most powerful organization of African Americans in the world. DuBois led the NAACP and edited its newspaper, *The Crisis.* He died in 1963.

Chapter Six:
Hard Times

In 1920, Garvey was more famous than ever. People all across America knew who he was. Not everybody agreed with his ideas, however. Many white people did not like him because he wanted to give power to African Americans. And many black people did not agree with him because he wanted blacks to move to Africa instead of staying where they are and fighting for change.

One African American who disagreed with Garvey was W.E.B. DuBois. DuBois was famous as the head of the powerful group called the National Association for the Advancement of Colored People. This group worked to win equal rights for African Americans. DuBois and his followers thought that black people and white people should be equal and live side by side. He did not agree with Garvey's idea that black people should have their own nation separate from white people.

African Church

Garvey also wanted African Americans to have their own church. He often told them they should not worship a god who looked like a white man. He said that since the Bible says God created man in his own image, a black god must have created Africans. Garvey formed his own church, the African Orthodox Church.

Instead of winning more followers, however, his church made some enemies for Garvey. At the time, some of the most powerful black people in America were ministers and other church leaders. Garvey tried to tell these leaders that they needed to switch to his African Orthodox Church. He said this would prove they were true Africans. The church leaders did not agree with this and began to speak badly of Garvey in their churches.

Angering African Americans

In 1921 Garvey did something that made many more African Americans dislike him. He met with the leader of the **Ku Klux Klan (KKK).** The KKK is a group that **discriminates** against people who are not white and Christian. KKK members did things like burn down the houses and churches of African Americans. They said they hated African Americans and sometimes they even killed them. Only a small percentage of white people actually belonged to the KKK, but many white people agreed with their ideas and supported them. Because of this, the group was still very powerful.

These Ku Klux Klan members in official KKK robes and hoods are meeting at Stone Mountain in Georgia in 1921.

Garvey met with the **KKK** leader because he thought it would help convince white people to support his ideas. He told KKK members that their ideas were not much different from his own. They both wanted blacks and whites to live in separate communities. This made many black people in America angry at Garvey. They could not understand how he could meet with people who hated African Americans. After Garvey met with the KKK leader, many black people in America stopped listening to him and left the **UNIA.**

Garvey had a difficult time in his home life in the early 1920s. He and his first wife got divorced. In 1922, he married his second wife, Amy Jacques.

Trouble with the Law

Meanwhile, Garvey was having trouble with the government. Garvey thought some people in the government did not like him only because he was a well-known black man. This was probably true, because in the 1920s, there were some racist people in the government, too. However, whether or not they were racist, others really thought Garvey was breaking the law. They said it was against the law for Garvey to sell stock in his company when it was **bankrupt.**

In 1922, the U.S. government arrested Garvey for cheating people in business. There was a trial in court. Garvey acted as his

Handcuffed, Garvey is seen here leaving court with officers of the law.

MARCUS GARVEY MUST GO!

Four of the Greatest Negro Meetings Ever Held in New York,

Sundays — August 6th, 13th, 20th and 27th
SHUFFLE INN MUSIC PARLORS

This poster was made by people who did not agree with Garvey's actions and beliefs. They wanted him to be put in jail or forced to leave the United States.

own lawyer. He tried to explain that he did not mean to cheat people. He said he was only trying to raise money for his cause. Garvey's trial lasted for almost one year, and Garvey was found guilty in 1924. He had to pay $1,000 and was sent to prison for five years.

Garvey did not have to go to prison right away because he **appealed** the court's decision. To appeal means to ask the court to consider your case again. Meanwhile, Garvey was free until he had to go back to court. Then, his case would be discussed again.

Garvey continued to run **UNIA.** He also continued to run the Black Star Shipping Line, but the company kept losing money. At

An African American supporter of the UNIA stands outside of a UNIA office in New York City in 1929. Garvey ran the UNIA from prison from 1924 until 1927, when his followers convinced the U.S. government to release him.

the same time, many African Americans were still angry with Garvey for doing things like meeting with the **KKK** leader.

In 1924, Garvey's case went to court again. He was found guilty again. This time he had to go to prison. He went to prison in Atlanta in 1925, at the age of 37.

Support in Prison

While Garvey was in prison, his supporters stood behind him. They wrote letters to leaders around the country asking for Garvey to be released. Many people visited him in prison. Many newspaper reporters wrote articles about him.

Some people felt that Garvey had been arrested unfairly. They said he did not really mean to commit a crime, he was just a bad businessman. They asked the government to **pardon** him. To pardon means to excuse someone for a crime and let them out of prison.

In 1927, Garvey's followers finally convinced the government to pardon him. In November of that year, President Calvin Coolidge signed his pardon. Garvey had been in prison for two years and nine months.

President Calvin Coolidge, who served from 1923 to 1927, agreed to pardon Garvey.

Garvey was released from prison, but he was not allowed to stay in the United States. This was because he was not a citizen of the United States. When people who are not citizens are convicted of crimes, they are often made to leave the country. This is called **deportation.** Garvey was not even allowed to visit **UNIA** offices in New York. He was sent straight from prison back to Jamaica.

Garvey stands in a military uniform, holding a sword. After he was released from prison, he returned to Jamaica.

Chapter Seven:
Final Years

The people of Jamaica gave Garvey a big welcome when he returned in 1927. They treated him like a hero. The crowd that gathered was the largest crowd of Jamaicans ever. Garvey was happy to be treated this way after being in prison.

Garvey got right to work back in Jamaica. He set up new **UNIA** offices. Soon he opened UNIA offices in other countries in the Caribbean and Central America. He still had many followers, but not as many as he had had a few years earlier.

Less than one year after he returned to Jamaica, Garvey and his wife moved to London, England. In London, Garvey opened another UNIA office, but not many people wanted to join his group there. Disappointed by the reaction in London to his message, Garvey returned to Jamaica with his wife in 1929. They soon had two sons named Marcus Jr. and Julius.

Back in Jamaica

Back in Jamaica again, Garvey kept working to raise money and support for **UNIA.** Later in 1929, he held the sixth yearly International **Convention** of the Negro People of the World. Just like the first convention in New York City in 1920, this one had bands, parades, and many meetings. Again, people from all over the world attended.

Also in 1929, Garvey started a new newspaper called *The Black Man.* He used this newspaper to get his message to people of African descent around the Caribbean and the world. He wrote that his old co-workers in New York had not been loyal to him. By now Garvey had split from the New York UNIA that he had started almost ten years earlier. Many black people around the world still saw Garvey as their leader. However, he lost many of his American followers once he left the United States.

Until now, Garvey had been a leader, but he had never held a government office. Now that Garvey was back in Jamaica, he became interested in Jamaican government. At that time Jamaica had a council that was similar to the U.S. Congress. It was made up of elected people from around the country. These people made the laws of Jamaica, and Garvey wanted to help make laws. He wanted to make laws that would help poor black Jamaicans have a better life.

Garvey became active in the Jamaican government in the late 1920s and early 1930s.
He tried to improve the lives of black people living in Jamaica.

Garvey ran for election to the council and won. He served on
the council for several terms, but as the years went by fewer people
looked up to him. Black people in Jamaica were getting poorer
instead of better off. Garvey was not able to help them, so they
stopped listening to him.

Garvey's ideas and message of black pride and black unity are still remembered today. A marcher can be seen carrying a picture of Marcus Garvey at the "Million Man March" in Washington, D.C., 1995.

Back to England

In 1935 Garvey and his wife and sons moved back to London. Garvey had very few followers left by then. In London, he still gave many speeches, but they were mostly on street corners. People were beginning to forget who he was. However, Garvey continued his work. He continued to publish his newspaper *The Black Man*, and he continued to talk about his dream of people of African descent from around the world returning to Africa. He traveled to

Canada and set up **UNIA** offices there. He wanted to visit the United States, but the government would not allow it.

In January of 1940, when Garvey was 53 years old, he had a stroke. A stroke happens when a blood vessel in the brain suddenly breaks or is blocked, preventing oxygen from getting to part of the brain. Worn out from a lifetime of fighting for his cause, Garvey could not recover from the stroke. He died on June 10, 1940.

Legend

Garvey was not very famous at the time of his death, but he left a large legacy. People around the world have not forgotten his powerful ideas about giving strength and pride back to black people.

Today there are still signs of Garvey's influence around the world. The red, green, and black flag that he designed is proudly flown around the world. Many black people wear these colors to show their **unity** with other people of African descent. Many popular movements since Garvey have borrowed his theme of black pride and black unity. His saying, "Black is beautiful," is heard in communities around the world.

Even people who do not agree with some of Garvey's ideas, such as moving back to Africa, agree that he was a great leader for his time. He gave something very valuable to black people all over the world. He made them feel proud to be black at a time when they were treated unfairly because of the color of their skin.

Glossary

appeal   to ask the court to consider your case again

bankrupt   company that has run out of money

colonialism   system in which a more powerful country takes over another country and governs it as if it belonged to the more powerful country

convention   large gathering of people interested in the same ideas. Usually includes a series of meetings, and sometimes lasts many days

deportation   act of being sent out of a country by the government. Often people convicted of crimes are deported from countries, and they are not allowed to return.

discriminate   to treat someone unfairly because of his or her appearance or qualities

discrimination   act of treating someone or being treated unfairly because of appearance or other qualities a person is born with

Harlem Renaissance   revival in black culture in Harlem during the 1920s. During this time, the neighborhood produced many famous black writers, musicians, and thinkers.

Ku Klux Klan (KKK)   group that discriminates and acts out against people who are not white and Christian

migrant workers   workers who travel around to find jobs

pardon   to excuse someone from a crime that the court said they were guilty of. People who are pardoned are released from jail before their sentence is up.

poverty   state of being very poor and not being able to afford the most basic things needed to live

printing press   machine used to print books and newspapers

race riots   large, violent fights between black people and white people in cities across the United States

revolt   people fighting against a government or an authority

segregation   in the United States, actions and rules that separated African-American people from white people

strike   employees refusing to work because they disagree with their employer over pay or working conditions

unite   to gather or link together under a common cause

United Negro Improvement Association (UNIA)   group founded by Garvey with the aim of helping black people help themselves by overcoming discrimination

unity   idea of joining together to be more powerful. Garvey believed in black unity.

Timeline

1887 – Marcus Mosiah Garvey is born in St. Anne's Bay, Jamaica.

1899 – Garvey's father dies.

1901 – Leaves school to learn to be a printer.

1903 – Moves to Jamaica and works in a print shop.

1910 – Leaves Jamaica for first time to find work in Costa Rica; travels around Central America for almost two years.

1912 – Goes to London, England, for the first time; meets many powerful African leaders.

1914 – Returns to Jamaica, starts the **Universal Negro Improvement Association (UNIA).**

1916 – Moves to United States; soon moves UNIA offices to New York City.

1919 – Begins newspaper called *Negro World*; marries Amy Ashwood.

1920 – Starts Black Star Shipping Line; holds first annual International Convention of the Negro People of the World.

1921 – Meets with **Ku Klux Klan** leader.

1922—Arrested for fraud (cheating people in business); divorces Amy Ashwood on June 15; marries Amy Jacques on July 27.

1925 – Goes to prison.

1927 – **Pardoned** by President Calvin Coolidge and sent back to Jamaica.

1930—Garvey's first son, also named Marcus, is born on September 17.

1933—Garvey's second son, Julius Winston Garvey, is born on August 16.

1940 – Marcus Garvey dies in London, England.

Further Information

Further reading

Archer, Jules. *They Had a Dream: the Civil Rights Struggle from Frederick Douglass to Marcus Garvey to Martin Luther King and Malcom X.* New York: Viking, 1993.

Altman, Susan. *Extraordinary African-Americans: From Colonial to Contemporary Times.* New York: Children's Press, 2001.

Rennert, Richard, ed. *Shapers of America: Profiles of Great Black Americans.* New York: Chelsea House Publishers, 1993.

Addresses

The Marcus Garvey and UNIA Papers Project
280 Kinsey Hall, UCLA
Los Angeles, California 90024

Marcus Garvey Library
27 Old Gloucester Street
London WC1N 3XX

Schomburg Center for Research in Black Culture
515 Malcolm X Boulevard
New York, NY 10037-1801

Index